For Luna Violet

BLOOMSBURY CHILDREN'S BOOKS
Bloomsbury Publishing Plc
50 Bedford Square, London, WC1B 3DP, UK
29 Earlsfort Terrace, Dublin 2, Ireland

BLOOMSBURY, BLOOMSBURY CHILDREN'S BOOKS and the Diana logo are
trademarks of Bloomsbury Publishing Plc

First published in Great Britain 2022 by Bloomsbury Publishing Plc

A catalogue record for this book is available from the British Library

ISBN: HB: 978-1-5266-1991-4 PB: 978-1-5266-1990-7 eBook: 978-1-5266-1989-1

2 4 6 8 10 9 7 5 3 1

Printed and bound in China by Leo Paper Products, Heshan, Guangdong

To find out more about our authors and books visit www.bloomsbury.com and sign up for our
newsletters.To find out more about Katie Abey visit www.katieabey.co.uk

WE FEEL HAPPY!

KATIE ABEY

BLOOMSBURY
CHILDREN'S BOOKS
LONDON OXFORD NEW YORK NEW DELHI SYDNEY

How are you feeling?

We are ALL made up of lots of different emotions. Sometimes they are feelings that make us feel GREAT and sometimes they make us feel not so good. Whether you are feeling super HAPPY or a little bit SAD, it is Ok to feel these feelings. In fact, EVERYONE around you has probably felt how you are feeling before.

There are a RAINBOW of emotions to explore so ... let's find out how the animals are feeling today!

Do you feel HAPPY when playing with your favourite toy?

Are you EXCITED about going to a party?

Does brushing your teeth make you feel GRUMPY?

Perhaps you don't KNOW how you are feeling ...

Are you SCARED because you had a bad dream?

We Feel Worried

Why do the animals feel worried?

Can we be friends?

We sometimes worry about meeting new people

YES!

I don't know why I feel worried

Talking to someone can help

What do you think your worry looks like? Can you draw it?

Drawing our worries can make them feel smaller

That's ok. Anything spilled can be cleared up.

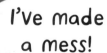

I've made a mess!

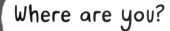

Where are you?

Over here!

We can feel worried when away from loved ones

TALENT SHOW

I've forgotten something!

We can share!

You can do it!

Take your time!

Can I help you?

You can help others when they feel worried

What makes YOU feel less worried?

I feel worried sometimes.

Me too!

Me three! It feels like I have butterflies in my tummy.

We all feel worried sometimes

We Feel Calm

What are the animals doing to feel **calm**?

We Feel Excited

Yippee! Hooray! What are the animals looking forward to today?

We Feel Scared

Why do the animals feel **scared**?

There's a a storm

But soon there will be a rainbow

I don't like the loud noises

Look at the pretty colours

Focus on the positives

what's that noise?

I'm scared

I haven't jumped before!

You can do it!

We all feel scared sometimes

I'm scared of spiders!

Look closer, he's friendly!

We Feel Curious

What are the animals **curious** about?

I'm reading about animals in a book

Why are carrots orange?

What's that noise?

We pretend to be things that make us curious

What's under there?

I'm curious about colours

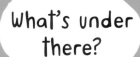

We Feel Sad

Why are the animals feeling sad?

Sometimes we cry when we feel sad

Sometimes we feel sad for no reason

I lost my teddy

What happens when we feel sad?

I'll share with you

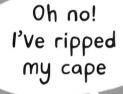

Oh no! I've ripped my cape

I hurt myself

You can borrow mine!

I'll patch you up in no time!

My toy is broken

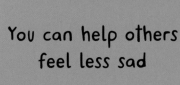

You can help others feel less sad

We Feel Grumpy

What's making the animals so cross?

It's TOO loud!

I don't want to brush my teeth

We're bored

I'm HUNGRY!

Sometimes we feel grumpy when we lose

We can feel grumpy when we're jealous

Grumpy

I don't like brushing my mane

I don't want to wash my hands

Are you ok?

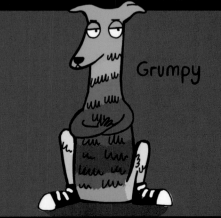

Grumpy

There are no cookies left!

We feel grumpy when we're tired

Feeling grumpy can make us feel cross

Making music together is fun

Let's dance while brushing our teeth!

How can YOU make yourself feel less grumpy?

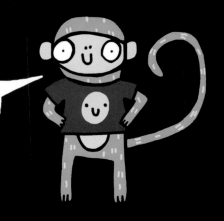

Exercise can make us less grumpy

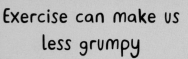

Having a snack can make us feel less grumpy

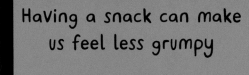

I'm happy you won this time

Yay for ice cream

Pose like an animal!

Let's make it fun

See how many bubbles you can make

Sometimes all you need is a hug

Yoga makes me feel less grumpy

You can share mine

Have you tried having a cat nap?

Take a deep breath and count

Let's talk about FEELINGS

Everyone has feelings, and it is important to talk about them. How can we help as parents and caregivers?

HAPPY

Asking your child to create a happiness recipe is a lovely way to help cook up some joy.
✦ A spoonful of hugs
✦ A cup of dancing
✦ A shake of fresh air
✦ Add the hugs and dancing together and mix with a shake of fresh air. Share with a special person.

What will YOU include?

WORRIED

Create a 'worry jar'. Find a container with a lid and encourage your child to write a note or draw a picture of any worries they may have to put in the jar. Encourage them to 'put their worries away' for a little while and go and do something different. You can come back and read the worries later, talking about whether that worry has now passed.

CALM

Talking to your child about what makes you calm can help them feel calm too. This might be something very simple like stroking a pet, having a cup of tea or spending time with friends and family. Can your child tell (or show) you something that makes them calm?

EXCITED

Recognising that excitement is an emotion can help children to learn about other feelings too. If you spot that your child is jumping up and down with excitement about going to a friend's party, you could say 'I can see that you're jumping for joy about going to see your friend. You must be feeling excited!' This technique can be used with all types of emotions and helps children to recognise their feelings.

SHY

We can help put children at ease by sharing our own experiences of being shy. Talking about a time in your life where you felt shy helps your child realise this is a normal emotion. Talk about what you did to feel better and ask them what they could do if a friend was feeling shy.

SCARED

Getting scared is a normal part of child development. You could ask your child to draw a picture of someone who is scared, and then talk about what has made them scared, and how you could help them.

CURIOUS

It's fun to go on a treasure hunt around the house, looking for things that you are curious about. When your child finds something, encourage them to find out more about it by looking up information or asking someone.

SAD

When your child is sad, they could think about a story or television programme where something sad happened. How did that character show they were sad - did they cry? Or did they go very quiet? Explore ways that you might help that person - perhaps they need a hug, or someone to talk to.

GRUMPY

We can help children understand their feelings by giving real life comparisons. Children can think about grumpiness as feeling like a bottle of fizzy pop. If you shake the bottle, all the bubbles fizz up inside it, so it needs some time to sit quietly and allow the bubbles to settle. If it doesn't sit quietly, there might be a BIG explosion when it's opened.

SORRY

Children could use two toys to role play what might happen when friends fall out and are upset over something. Talk about possible solutions and how they might both be feeling. How could you avoid this happening in the future?